A. Dunlop Gordon

Nuggets of Gold from Memory's Mine

A. Dunlop Gordon

Nuggets of Gold from Memory's Mine

ISBN/EAN: 9783337294007

Printed in Europe, USA, Canada, Australia, Japan

Cover: Foto ©Thomas Meinert / pixelio.de

More available books at **www.hansebooks.com**

Nuggets of Gold

FROM

Memory's Mine.

BY

A. DUNLOP GORDON.

Out of evil cometh good.
Out of darkness cometh light.

———

From that rich mine how often hast thou brought
The pure and precious pearls of splendid thought.

PHILADELPHIA.

1894.

PREFACE.

THE following minute nosegays coined in the mint of language are neither extracts nor are they original, but were culled for their fragrance and stored away in memory's storehouse, welling up at times as memory serves them without reference to their original form. The first I indite in remembrance of a deceased brother. The lines were written in pencil on a piece of paper and found under his pillow after his death.

NUGGETS OF GOLD.

On ! most delightful hour by man
    Experienced here below,
The hour which terminates his span,
    His folly, and his woe.

Worlds would not bribe me back to tread
    Again life's dreary waste,
To see again my day o'erspread
    With all the gloomy past.

My home henceforth is in the skies ;
    Earth, sea, and sun adieu,
All heaven unfolded to my eyes,
    I have no sight for you.

Existence is a long-drawn sigh after repose, which is nowhere to be found in this world except through the blood of Jesus.

Come unto me, all ye ends of the earth, and be ye saved, for I am God, and besides me there is none other.

I will instruct you in the way thou shalt go. I will guide thee with mine eye.

> For I am the way, the truth, the life,
>   No son of human race,
> But such as I conduct and guide
>   Shall see my Father's face.

Fear not, for I am with thee; be not dismayed, for I am thy God: I will strengthen thee; yea, I will uphold you by the right hand of my righteousness.

> He died to bear the guilt of men,
>   That sins might be forgiven;
> He lives to bless them and defend,
>   And plead their cause in heaven.

Oh, what a manifestation of love is here! That the Son of God should take our great debt upon Him and assume our place. Yes, it is love indeed, unutterable, unfathomable love.

> Wouldst thou follow Him to glory,
>   And His joys and triumphs share,
> Then through nights' long dreary watches
>   Wrestle on in secret prayer.

There is no means of grace so enriching to the soul as private prayer. It is a golden pipe through which the Lord is graciously pleased to convey spiritual blessings to the soul. He knoweth all our wants, and without our asking Him could supply us at the best possible time.

Though the Lord will never remember the sins of a believer to his condemnation, yet the believer himself will always remember them to his humiliation.

O Lord, enlighten my understanding that I may know Thee, sanctify my affections that I may love Thee, and put Thy fear into my heart that I may dread to offend Thee. Wean my affections, O Lord, from the things of this world, and whatever my state and condition may be here, give me grace therewith to be content.

> When the waves of trouble heighten,
> When the billows fiercely foam,
> All you see conspires to frighten,
> Friends and helpers fail to come.
>
> When of human aid despairing,
> And no voice the tempest calms,
> Think of this, that underneath you
> Are the " Everlasting Arms."

Be not deceived; God is not mocked: for whatsoever a man soweth, that shall he also reap. If he sow to the flesh he shall of the flesh reap

corruption, and if he sow to the Spirit he shall of
the Spirit reap life everlasting.

I am a monument of God's mercy and for-
bearance.

> When in the slippery paths of youth
>   With heedless steps I ran,
> Thine Arms unseen conveyed me forth,
>   And led me up to man.
>
> Through hidden dangers, toils, and death
>   He gently cleared the way,
> And through the pleasing snares of vice,
>   More to be feared than they.
>
> Through every period of my life
>   Thy goodness I'll proclaim,
> And after death in distant worlds
>   Resume the glorious theme.

Neither do I condemn thee; go and sin no more.

Fear not, for I have redeemed thee, I have
called thee by thy name, thou art mine. When
thou passest through the waters, I will be with
thee; and through the rivers, they shall not over-
flow thee; when thou walkest through the fire,
thou shalt not be burned; neither shall the flame
kindle upon thee.

I am with you alway, even unto the end of the world.

> Look unto me ; 'tis no great deed
> A humble look to cast ;
> This is enough, the power that saves
> Is mine from first to last.

Our journey is through a trackless desert ; we know not a foot of the road ; all before us is untrodden path ; the road is lined with snares and dangers. There are many by-paths.

> Lead, Saviour, lead amid the encircling gloom,
> Lead Thou me on ;
> The night is dark, and I am far from home,
> Lead Thou me on.
> Keep Thou my feet ; I do not ask to see
> The distant scene ; one step enough for me.

Come unto me, all ye that are heavy laden, and I will give you rest. My yoke is easy, my burden is light. Come buy wine and milk, without money and without price. Come unto Him just as thou art, and He will make you what thou shouldst be. He counsels thee to buy of Him the gold of faith and the garment of salvation. Take Him now at His gospel word. The poorer thou art the better ; the oil of His grace flows most abundantly into empty vessels.

I heard the voice of Jesus say,
   Come unto me and rest;
Lay down, thou weary one, lay down
   Thy head upon my breast.

I came to Jesus as I was,
   Weary and worn and sad;
I found in Him a resting-place,
   And He has made me glad.

The shortest way out of every difficulty is to
carry it at once to Jesus, who is the opener of the
seven seals.

Hast thou within a care so deep
It chases from thine eyelids sleep?
To thy Redeemer take that care,
And change anxiety to prayer.

Prayer is the application of want to Him who
alone can relieve it, the confession of sin to Him
who alone can pardon it.

The heart knoweth its own bitterness.

Enter into thy closet, and when thou hast shut
thy door, pray to thy Father which is in secret.

O Thou, by whom we come to God,
   The life, the truth, the way,
The path of prayer thyself hast trod;
   Lord, teach us how to pray.

He that covereth his sins shall not prosper, but whoso confesseth and forsaketh them shall have mercy. The eyes of the Lord are over the righteous, and His ears are open to their prayers.

> O for a closer walk with God,
>   A calm and heavenly frame ;
> A light to shine upon the road
>   That leads me to the Lamb.

Many good and benevolent men are just now passing away, in our midst (G. W. C.) one known throughout the world ; as Paul said, so may it be said of him : " I have fought a good fight, I have finished my course, I have kept the faith : henceforth there is laid up for me a crown of righteousness, which the Lord, the righteous judge, shall give me at that day."   .

> The race appointed I have run,
> The combat's o'er, the prize is won ;
> And now my witness is on high,
> And now my record's in the sky.

> Jesus, how glorious is thy grace !
>   When in Thy name we trust,
> Our faith receives a righteousness
>   That makes the sinner just.

Here we have no continuing city, but we seek one to come.

Dost thou not feel that thou art saved to live?
　Dost thou not know that thou art saved to save?
Forgiven that thou mightest too forgive?
　Redeemed alike for both sides of the grave.

Thou shalt love the Lord thy God with all thy
heart, and with all thy soul, and with all thy mind.
This is the first and great commandment. And the
second is like unto it, Thou shalt love thy neigh-
bor as thyself. On these two commandments
hang all the law and the prophets.

> Go preach my gospel, saith the Lord;
> 　Bid the whole earth my grace receive;
> Explain to them my sacred word;
> 　Bid them believe, obey, and live.

For the Son of man shall come in the glory of
His Father with His angels, and then He shall
reward every man according to his works.

Eye hath not seen, nor ear heard, neither have
entered into the heart of man the things which
God hath prepared for them that love Him.

There remaineth a rest for the people of God.

> Till Jesus comes our labors must not cease;
> Our joys are joys of conquest, not of peace.

Blessed is the man that endureth trial, for when he is tried he shall receive the crown of life, which the Lord hath promised to them that love Him.

> Thrice happy they in tears who sow,
> To reap in joy and love,
> That drop their seed on earth below,
> And find their sheaves above.

We are made partakers of Christ if we hold the beginning of our confidence steadfast unto the end.

> Christian, when thy way seems darkest,
> When thine eyes with tears are dim,
> Straight to God thy Father hastening ;
> Tell thy troubles all to Him.

Cast thy burden upon the Lord and He will sustain you.

I need Thee, precious Jesus, for I am full of sin,
My soul is dark and guilty, my heart is dead within.
I need the cleansing fountain, where I can always
    flee,
The blood of Christ most precious the sinner's perfect
    plea.

Seek and possess holiness, and consolation will assuredly follow.

I will make an altar unto God, who answered me in the day of my distress, and was with me in the way which I went.

Pray without ceasing. It is not he who begins in the spirit and ends in the flesh, but he that endureth to the end that will be saved.

Before they call I will answer, and while they are yet speaking I will hear.

Honor the Lord with thy substance, and with the first fruits of all thine increase : so shall thy barns be filled with plenty, and thy presses shall burst out with new wine.

A man may as soon read the Scriptures without eyes as understand the mysteries of the Gospel without grace.

I am the living bread which came down from heaven : if any man eat of this bread, he shall live forever : and the bread that I will give is my flesh, which I will give for the life of the world.

Verily, verily, I say unto you, He that heareth my word, and believeth on Him that sent me, hath life eternal, and into the judgment he shall not come, but hath passed out of death into life.

With the heart man believeth unto righteousness, and with the mouth confession is made unto salvation.

Watch therefore, you know neither the day nor the hour wherein the Son of man cometh.

Hath He said it and shall He not do it? Hath He spoken and shall He not bring it to pass?

> A few more days, or weeks, or years
> In this dark valley to repine;
> A few more sighs, a few more tears,
> And we shall bid adieu to time.
>
> Billows of disappointment roll
> Along the restless tide of time,
> But gospel faith bears up the soul
> Till an eternal calm shall shine.

God is able to make all grace abound toward you, that ye always, having all-sufficiency in all things, may abound in every good work.

> O Lord, impress thine image on my soul;
> My will, my temper, and my tongue control;
> Lead me through life to gratify Thy grace,
> And after death to see Thee face to face.

Whosoever shall do the will of my Father which is in heaven, the same is my brother, my sister, and my mother.

As the branch cannot bear fruit of itself, except it abide in the vine; no more can ye, except ye abide in me.

Abide in Me! sinner so poor and weak,
Vain is each other refuge thou wouldst seek.
Hidden in Me, thy sins are seen no more ;
Blameless thou'lt stand the judgment seat before.

I must work the works of Him that sent me while it is day; the night cometh when no man can work.   The hand of the diligent maketh rich.

The work which His goodness began
    The arm of His strength will complete ;
His promise is Yea and Amen,
    And never was forfeited yet.

Only believe. Believe on the Lord Jesus Christ, and thou shalt be saved.

My grace is sufficient for you.

The world can never fill the heart of man, for the heart is three-cornered, and the world is round.

What shall it profit a man if he gain the whole world and lose his own soul? Or what shall a man give in exchange for his soul?

> O for a closer walk with God,
>   A calm and heavenly frame;
> A light to shine upon the road
>   That leads me to the Lamb.

Peace I leave with you, my peace I give unto you: not as the world giveth, give I unto you. Thou wilt keep him in perfect peace whose mind is stayed on Thee.

> I'll hear what God, the Lord, will say;
>   He will speak peace to me:
> Look unto Me and be ye saved,
>   I set the prisoner free.

Who can tell what a day or an hour may bring forth? Here we are. If we look back, we have a bright stream of light and knowledge. If we look forward, we look into darkness impenetrable to man. Only the great Jehovah, who knoweth the end from the beginning, and with whom there is no darkness at all. Eternity past and eternity to come, with all their teeming incidents, stand in His view a fixed unchangeable picture.

I see not a step before me
  As I tread on another year,
But the past is still in God's keeping,
  The future His mercy will clear,
And what looks dark in the distance
  May brighten as it draws near.

Whosoever shall confess me before men, him
will I confess also, before my Father which is in
heaven. Come now and be emancipated. He waits
to be gracious and the time is short; no one can
tell at what moment the voice of exhortation and
of love may be forever silenced.

O let me walk with Thee, Thou mighty one,
Lean on Thine arm and trust Thy love alone,
With Thee hold converse sweet where'er I go,
Thy smile of love my highest bliss below.

He that is not with me is against me. It is
good for me to draw near to God. Remember
me, O my God, for good.

We would see Jesus; all is gloom around us,
  Dark shadows falling from the years gone by,
The sins of other days, like phantoms rising,
  Lifting their hands for judgment to the sky.

I will not fail thee nor forsake thee.

For the Lord will have mercy on Jacob, and will yet choose Israel and set them in their own land.

> I am the First and I the Last,
> Through endless years the same;
> I am is my memorial still,
> And my eternal name.

Not every one that saith unto me, Lord, Lord, shall enter into the kingdom of heaven, but he that doeth the will of my Father, which is in heaven. Blessed are the poor in spirit, for theirs is the kingdom of heaven.

> Not in mine innocence I trust,
> I bow before Thee in the dust,
> And through my Saviour's blood alone
> I look for mercy at Thy throne.

Christ in you the Hope of glory; which Hope we have as an anchor of the soul, both sure and steadfast, and which entereth into that within the veil.

> Jesus, my Anchor, Refuge, Hope,
> My Saviour and my King,
> Through all life's dark and stormy waves
> To Thee, to Thee I cling.

Let me die the death of the righteous, and let my last end be like His.

O Lord, in mo thy mighty power oxert,
Enlighten, comfort, sanctify my heart,
Sweeten my temper and subdue my will,
Make me like Jesus, with Thy spirit fill.

I will lead them in paths they have not known ;
I will make darkness light before them, and
crooked things straight.   These things will I do
unto them, and not forsake them.

Lead me, my Father, lead Thy child,
    For I am blind and cannot see
One step through this dark, dreary wild,
    But I am safe while led by Thee.

As thy days so shall thy strength be.

One by one thy griefs shall meet thee ;
    Do not fear an armed band ;
One will fade as others greet thee,
    Shadows passing through the land.

He was wounded for our transgressions, He
was bruised for our iniquities.

I lay my sins on Jesus,
    The spotless Lamb of God ;
He bears them all and frees us
    From the accursed load.

If ye then, being evil, know how to give good gifts unto your children, how much more shall your heavenly Father give the Holy Spirit to them that ask Him.

> Blest Spirit! I would yield myself to Thee.
> Do for me more than I can ask or think.
> Let me Thy holy habitation be,
> And daily deeper from Thy fulness drink.

Blessed is the man whom Thou chastenest, O Lord, and teachest him out of Thy law. For He maketh sore, and bindeth up. He woundeth, and His hands make whole.

> I thank Thee for the trials, Lord,
> Which made me know myself and Thee:
> Myself, all weakness, Thee all power,
> Pity, and love to spend on me.

The cup which my Father has given me, shall I not drink it? In the hand of the Lord there is a cup. It is full of mixture.

> Dread not the cup of sorrow,
> Thy God that cup hath mixed.
> Think not of ills to-morrow,
> His love thy lot has fixed.

> Sing, for the days of sadness
> Are flying fast away.
> Sing, for the home of gladness
> Is nearing day by day.

What is our life? It is even a vapor that appeareth for a little time and then vanisheth away. Man that is born of a woman is of few days and full of trouble. He cometh forth as a flower and is cut down.

When memory reveals all the events of your past life, all the faithful warnings you have had, all the good books you have read, all the gospel sermons you have heard, all the secret stirrings and admonitions of God's Spirit with your soul, and have resisted and rejected all, what will your feelings be when death approaches?

> Let nothing keep you back from Christ,
> Nothing—without, within ;
> But spread at once before the Throne
> Your sorrows and your sin.

Repent ye, therefore, and be converted, that your sins may be blotted out when the time of refreshing shall come from the presence of the Lord, and He shall send Jesus Christ.

There is a Fountain filled with blood
    Drawn from Emmanuel's veins;
And sinners plunged beneath that flood
    Lose all their guilty stains.

Seek ye first the kingdom of God and His righteousness, and all these things will be added unto you. Acknowledge the Lord in all your ways, and He will direct your steps. He will be a lamp to thy feet and a light to thy path.

Lead, Saviour, lead amid the encircling gloom,
        Lead Thou me on;
The night is dark, and I am far from home,
        Lead Thou me on.
Keep Thou my feet; I do not ask to see
The distant scene; one step enough for me.

The sacrifice of God is a broken spirit, a broken and a contrite heart.

He that cometh to me shall never hunger, and he that believeth on me shall never thirst.

I was wandering and weary
    When the Saviour came unto me;
For the paths of sin were dreary,
    And the world had ceased to woo me;
And I thought I heard him say,
As He came along His way:

3

Wandering souls, oh, do come near me !
My sheep should never fear me ;
I am the Shepherd true.

Thou wilt show me the path of life: in Thy presence is fulness of joy; at Thy right hand there are pleasures for evermore.

God is our refuge and strength, a very present help in trouble.

Wait on the Lord and He shall exalt thee to inherit the land.

My grace is sufficient for you.   We walk by faith, not by sight.

Oh, eyes that are weary and hearts that are sore,
Look off unto Jesus, and sorrow no more.
The light of His countenance shineth so bright,
That on earth, as in heaven, there need be no night.

I will not leave you comfortless ; I will come unto you.

In the time of trouble He shall hide me in His Pavilion, in the secret of His Tabernacle shall He hide me.   He shall set me upon a Rock.

Eye hath not seen, nor ear heard, neither have entered into the heart of man, the things which God hath prepared for them that love Him.

Though your sins be as scarlet, they shall be white as snow; though red like crimson, they shall be as wool.

If we confess our sins, God is righteous and just to forgive us our sins and cleanse us from all unrighteousness.

That man no guard or weapon needs
  Whose heart the blood of Jesus knows;
But safe may pass, if duty leads,
  Through burning sands and mountain snows.

Released from guilt he knows no fear;
  Redemption is his shield and tower;
He sees his Maker always near
  To help in every trying hour.

Lo! I am with thee alway, even unto the end of the world.

A few more years shall roll,
  A few more seasons come,
And we shall be with those that rest
  Asleep within the tomb.

Then, O my Lord, prepare
My soul for that great day ;
Oh, wash me in Thy precious Blood
And take my sins away.

I am the Resurrection and the Life ; he that
believeth in me, though he were dead, yet shall
he live.

And man forsakes this earthly scene,
Ah ! never to return ;
Can any following spring revive
The ashes of the urn ?

Him that overcometh will I make a pillar in
the temple of my God, and he shall no more go
out.

Just as thou art, without one trace
Of love, or joy, or inward grace,
Or meetness for the heavenly place,
O guilty sinner, come !

Thy sins I bore on Calvary's tree,
The stripes thy due were laid on Me,
That peace and pardon might be free,
O wretched sinner, come !

Thou wilt keep him in perfect peace whose
mind is stayed on Thee.

All things work together for good to them that love God, to them who are the called according to His purpose.

When my heart is overwhelmed within me, lead me to the Rock that is higher than I. Why art thou cast down, O my soul? and why art thou disquieted within me? hope thou in God: for I shall yet praise Him, who is the health of my countenance and my God.

A bruised reed shall He not break, and smoking flax shall He not quench.

> Trust in the Lord, forever trust,
> And banish all your fears;
> Strength in the Lord Jehovah is
> Eternal as His years.

Open Thou mine eyes, that I may behold wondrous things out of Thy law. Sanctify me through Thy truth; Thy word is truth.

Search me, O God, and know my heart; try me, and know my thoughts, and see if there be any wicked way in me, and lead me in the way everlasting.

The Lord gave, and the Lord hath taken away ;
blessed be the name of the Lord.   Enable me to
bear patiently whatever trials may be allotted me,
firmly trusting in Thy word that all things shall
work together for good to them that love Thee.

> One sweetly solemn thought
>   Comes to me o'er and o'er ;
> I'm nearer Home to-day
>   Than ever I have been before.
>
> Nearer my Father's House,
>   Where the many mansions be ;
> Nearer the great White Throne,
>   Nearer the Jasper Sea.
>
> 'Tis God that lifts our comforts high,
>   Or sinks them in the grave ;
> He gives, and when He takes away,
>   He takes but what He gave.

Lord, I am oppressed, undertake for me.   In all
my ways may I acknowledge Thee, and do Thou
in mercy direct my path.

> He who leads me knows the pathway,
>   Every step Himself has planned ;
> Sees the end from the beginning,
>   Let me only feel His Hand.

Jesus, I love to trace,
Throughout the sacred page,
The footsteps of Thy grace,
The same in every age.
Oh, grant that I may faithful be
To clearer light vouchsafed to me !

Behold, the husbandman waiteth for the precious fruit of the earth, and hath long patience for it, until he receive the early and latter rain. Be ye also patient; stablish your hearts : for the coming of the Lord draweth nigh.

There is a world we have not seen,
Which time shall never dare destroy,
Where mortal footstep hath not been,
Nor ear hath caught its sound of joy.

Walk in love, as Christ also hath loved us, and hath given Himself for us. And now abideth Faith, Hope, Charity ; but the greatest of these is Charity.

My Saviour, God, who gavest Thy life for me,
Let nothing come between my heart and Thee.
From Thee no thought, no secret would I keep,
But on Thy breast my tears of anguish weep.

The Lord is nigh unto them that are of a broken heart, and saveth such as be of a contrite spirit.

Thou on my head in early youth didst smile,
And though rebellious and perverse meanwhile,
Thou has not left me, oft as I left Thee.
On to the close, O Lord, abide with me.

Give me, O my God, a heart full of Christian
meekness and charity, that I may willingly forget
the evil I have received, and be always disposed
to do good to others.

Is there a good your heart can wish
That I've not bought for thee?
Take and enjoy what I have bought,
And find your all in Me.

Search me, O God, and know my heart; try
me and know my thoughts; and see if there be
any wicked way in me; and lead me in the way
everlasting.

Yes, I have loved thee with an everlasting love:
therefore with loving-kindness have I drawn thee.

I found this treasure at the Cross;
And there to every kind
Of weary, heavy-laden souls,
Christ gives a quiet mind.

What I do thou knowest not now, but thou
shalt know hereafter.

Whatever ye do, do all to the glory of God.

Think not many words you need
To make your meaning clear.
A look will carry all to Him;
A sigh will reach His ear.

Love not the world, neither the things that are
in the world. If any man love the world, the love
of the Father is not in him.

Lord Jesus, help me now to flee,
And seek my hope alone in Thee;
Apply Thy Blood, Thy Spirit give;
Subdue my sins, and let me live.

Life is a precious boon to mortals given,
Which, if well spent, will be renewed in heaven.

Life is at best but a tempestuous sea,
That fast rolls onward to Eternity.

When forced to part from those we love,
If sure to meet to-morrow,
We still a pang of anguish prove,
And feel a touch of sorrow.

But who can paint the briny tears
We shed when thus we sever,
If forced to part for months, for years,
To part, perhaps forever?

My mother's favorite hymn, and the last she ever repeated :

Where high the heavenly temple stands,
The house of God not made with hands,
A great High Priest our nature wears,
The guardian of mankind appears.

He who for men their surety stood,
And poured on earth His precious Blood,
Pursues in heaven His mighty plan,
The Saviour and the Friend of man.

Though now ascended up on high,
He bends on earth a brother's eye.
Partaker of the human name,
He knows the frailty of our frame.

Our Fellow-Sufferer yet retains
A fellow-feeling of our pains,
And still remembers in the skies
His tears, His agonies and cries.

In every pang that rends the heart
The Man of sorrows had a part.
He sympathizes with our grief,
And to the sufferer sends relief.

With boldness, therefore, at the Throne,
Let us make all our sorrows known,
And ask the aid of heavenly power
To help us in the evil hour.

Our life, how short ! a groan, a sigh ;
We live, and then begin to die ;
But oh ! how great a mercy this,
That death's a portal into bliss !

There is an hour of peaceful rest
  To mourning wanderers given ;
There is a joy for souls distressed,
A balm for every wounded breast ;
  'Tis found above in heaven.

There is a soft, a downy bed,
  'Tis fair as breath of even ;
A couch for weary mortals spread,
Where they may rest the aching head
  And find repose in heaven.

There is a home for weary souls
  By sin and sorrow driven,
When tossed on life's tempestuous shoals,
Where storms arise and oceans roll,
  And all is drear but heaven.

There Faith lifts up her cheerful eye
  To brighter prospects given,
And views the tempest passing by,
The evening shadows quickly fly,
  And all serene in heaven.

There fragrant flowers immortal bloom
  And joys supreme are given ;
There rays divine disperse the gloom,
Beyond the confines of the tomb
  Appears the dawn of heaven.

O Thou who driest the mourner's tear,
How dark this world would be
If, when deceived and wounded here,
We could not fly to Thee !

The friends who in our sunshine live,
When winter comes are flown,
And he who has but tears to give
Must weep those tears alone.

But Thou wilt heal that broken heart,
Which, like the plants that throw
Their fragrance from the wounded part,
Breathes sweetness out of woe.

When joy no longer soothes or cheers,
And e'en the hope that threw
A moment's sparkle o'er our tears,
Is dimmed and vanished too,

Oh, who could bear life's stormy doom
Did not Thy wing of love
Come brightly wafting through the gloom
One Peace-Branch from above ?

Then sorrow touched by Thee grows bright,
With more than rapture's ray,
As darkness shows us worlds of light
We never saw by day.

When gathering clouds around I view,
And days are dark, and friends are few,
On Him I lean, who, not in vain,
Experienced every human pain;
He sees my griefs, allays my fears,
And counts and treasures up my tears.

If aught should tempt my soul to stray
From heavenly wisdom's narrow way,
To fly the good I would pursue,
Or do the thing I would not do;
Still He who felt temptation's power
Shall guard me in that dangerous hour.

When vexing thoughts within me rise,
And, sore dismayed, my spirit dies,
Yet He who did vouchsafe to bear
The sickening anguish of despair
Shall sweetly soothe, shall gently dry,
The throbbing heart, the streaming eye.

When, mourning, o'er some stone I bend
Which covers all that was a friend,
And from his voice, his hand, his smile,
Divides me for a little while,
Thou, Saviour, mark'st the tears I shed,
For thou didst weep o'er Lazarus dead.

———

Jesus, I my cross have taken,
    All to leave and follow Thee;
Naked, poor, despised, forsaken,
    Thou from hence my all shalt be.

Perish every fond ambition,
   All I've sought, or hoped, or known ;
Yet how rich is my condition !
   God and heaven are still my own.

Let the world despise and leave me,
   They have left my Saviour too ;
Human hearts and looks deceive me,
   Thou art not, like them, untrue.
And whilst Thou shalt smile upon me,
   God of wisdom, love, and might,
Foes may hate and friends may scorn me ;
   Show Thy face, and all is bright.

Go, then, earthly fame and treasure ;
   Come disaster, scorn, and pain ;
In Thy service pain is pleasure,
   With Thy favor loss is gain.
I have called Thee Abba, Father,
   I have set my heart on Thee ;
Storms may howl and clouds may gather,
   All must work for good to me.

Oh, draw me Saviour, after Thee,
   So shall I run and never tire ;
With gracious words still comfort me ;
   Be Thou my hope, my sole desire.
Free me from every weight, nor fear,
Nor sin can come, if Thou art here.

I feel it a pleasing duty to close this little book with the following hymn in memory of the most delightful old colonial lady it has been my privilege to meet. I had known her some years previous to her death, which took place in New York in 1868, at the age of ninety-six. She had been blind for over forty years, but her bright mind and sunshiny disposition, even to the end, cast rays of happiness over all. Her conversational powers were grand. She would occasionally speak of Washington's visits at her father's house, adding, " We girls never liked him, he always looked so stern at us." This, to me, is a pleasant feeling, that I knew one who had conversed with and known Washington personally. She came of the old Eastern Shore of Maryland stock, her father being a commodore of Revolutionary fame, her uncle, I believe, the first Secretary of the United States Treasury, and her two nephews in New York, who in their day rose to great financial fame. She repeated the hymn only a short time before her death.

> Vital spark of heavenly flame !
> Quit, oh, quit this mortal frame !
> Trembling, hoping, lingering, flying,
> Oh, the pain, the bliss of dying !
> Cease, fond nature, cease thy strife,
> And let me languish into life.

Hark! they whisper! angels say,
"Sister spirit, come away!"
What is this absorbs me quite,
Steals my senses, shuts my sight,
Drowns my spirit, draws my breath,—
Tell me, my soul, can this be death?

The world recedes, it disappears!
Heaven opens to my eyes! my ears
　With sounds seraphic ring!
Lend, lend your wings! I mount! I fly!
O Grave, where is thy victory?
　O Death, where is thy sting?

O Father, Almighty, to Thee be addressed,
With Christ and the Spirit, one God ever blessed,
All glory and worship from earth and from heaven,
As was, and is now, and shall ever be given.

FINIS.

www.ingramcontent.com/pod-product-compliance
Lightning Source LLC
Chambersburg PA
CBHW021451090426
42739CB00009B/1707